Oxford University Press, Great Clarendon Street, Oxford OX2 6DP

Oxford New York
Athens Auckland Bangkok Bogota Bombay
Buenos Aires Calcutta Cape Town Dar es Salaam
Delhi Florence Hong Kong Istanbul Karachi
Kuala Lumpur Madras Madrid Melbourne
Mexico City Nairobi Paris Singapore
Taipei Tokyo Toronto Warsaw

and associated companies in
Berlin Ibadan

Oxford is a trade mark of Oxford University Press

This selection and arrangement © John Foster 1996
Illustrations © Carol Thompson 1996
First published in this edition 1997
Reprinted 1998
First published in paperback 1998

A CIP catalogue record for this book is available
from the British Library

ISBN 0 19 276145 5 (hardback)
ISBN 0 19 276146 3 (paperback)

Printed in Hong Kong

First Verses

Finger Rhymes   Action Rhymes

Counting Rhymes   Chanting Rhymes

Compiled by John Foster
Illustrated by Carol Thompson

Oxford University Press

Oxford   New York   Toronto

Acknowledgements

We are grateful for permission to include the following poems in this collection:

John Agard: 'What Turkey Doing?' from *No Hickory No Dickery No Dock* by John Agard and Grace Nichols (Viking, 1991). Copyright © John Agard 1991, reprinted by permission of the author c/o Caroline Sheldon Literary Agency. **Marie Brookes:** 'Creepy Crawly Creatures', Copyright © Marie Brookes 1996, first published in this collection, by permission of the author. **Wendy Cope:** 'Teeth' and 'If I had a ten pence piece' (retitled 'If I Had a Silver Coin' with the author's agreement) both from *Twiddling Your Thumbs: Hand Rhymes* by Wendy Cope, reprinted by permission of the publishers, Faber & Faber Ltd. **Delphine Evans:** 'Caterpillar' from *Fingers, Feet & Fun,* written and compiled by Delphine Evans (Hutchinson), reprinted by permission of Random House UK Ltd. **Eric Finney:** 'Countdown', Copyright © Eric Finney 1996, first published in this collection by permission of the author. **Sheree Fitch:** 'Mabel Murple' from *Toes in My Nose,* Copyright © 1987 by Sheree Fitch, reprinted by permission of the publishers, Doubleday Canada Limited. **John Foster:** 'Letters', 'Marty Smarty', 'Here a Bear, There a Bear', and adaption of traditional Caribbean poem 'One, Two, Three, Four', Copyright © John Foster 1996, first published in this collection. 'When Susie's Eating Custard', from *Food Poems* compiled by John Foster (OUP, 1993), 'Dinosaur Dreams' from *Dinosaur Poems* compiled by John Foster (OUP, 1983), both poems Copyright © John Foster 1993. 'Walking Round the Zoo' from *Themes for Early Years: Myself,* compiled by Irene Yates (Scholastic, 1995), and 'Letter Shapes' (first published with the title 'Point with your finger') from *Themes for Early Years: Shapes,* compiled by Irene Yates (Scholastic, 1995), both poems Copyright © John Foster 1995. All poems used by permission of the author. **Carolyn Graham:** 'One, Two, I Like You', 'All Good Dogs', 'Birds in the Birdcage', and 'One Little Kitten', Copyright © Carolyn Graham 1996, first published in this collection by permission of the author. 'Little Amanda Sat on a Panda' from *Mother Goose Jazz Chants* by Carolyn Graham, Copyright © 1995 by Oxford University Press, reprinted by permission of the publishers. **Babs Bell Hajdusiewicz:** 'Finger Play' and 'Squirmy Earthworm', first published in *Poetry Works! The First Verse,* collection © 1993 by Modern Curriculum Press, reprinted by permission of the author. **Linda Hammond:** 'Monsters' and 'Exercises' from *One Blue Boat* by Linda Hammond, Copyright © Linda Hammond 1991, (first published by Viking Children's Books, 1991), and 'The Robot' from *Five Furry Teddy Bears* by Linda Hammond, Copyright © Linda Hammond 1990, (Puffin, 1990), reprinted by permission of Penguin Books Ltd. **Barbara Ireson:** 'Balloon' from *Over and Over Again,* edited by Barbara Ireson and Christopher Rowe (Hutchinson), reprinted by permission of Random House UK Ltd. **Tony Langham:** 'See These Fingers', Copyright © Tony Langham 1996, first published in this collection by permission of the author. **Daphne Lister:** 'Hats', Copyright © Daphne Lister 1996, first published in this collection by permission of the author. **Tony Mitton:** 'Counting Couples', 'Beach Counting', 'Rocket', 'That One's Me!', 'The Crop Song', 'Lazy Little Alligator', 'The Bird', 'Seaside Song', 'Firework', 'Arabian Nights', and 'The Slide', Copyright © Tony Mitton 1996, first published in this collection by permission of the author. **Jack Ousbey:** 'Five Little Fingers' and 'This Finger's Straight', Copyright © Jack Ousbey 1996, first published in this collection by permission of the author. **Brian Patten:** 'Squeezes' from *Gargling With Jelly* by Brian Patten, Copyright © Brian Patten 1985, (first published by Viking Children's Books, 1985), reprinted by permission of Penguin Books Ltd. **Joan Poulson:** 'Three Purple Elephants', Copyright © Joan Poulson 1996, first published in this collection by permission of the author. **Jack Prelutsky:** One verse of 'Spaghetti! Spaghetti!' from *Rainy Day Saturday* by Jack Prelutsky, Copyright © 1980 by Jack Prelutsky, reprinted by permission of Greenwillow Books, a division of William Morrow and Company, Inc. **John Rice:** 'Monkey Tricks' from *Bears Don't Like Bananas* by John Rice, Copyright © John Rice 1991, reprinted by permission of Macdonald Young Books. **Michael Rosen:** 'I Don't Like Custard', from *Never Mind* by Michael Rosen, reprinted by permission of the publishers, Longman Group Ltd. **Nancy Byrd Turner:** 'Sing a Song of Popcorn' extract from 'A Popcorn Song' in *Sing a Song of Popcorn* edited by Beatrice Schenk de Regniers *et al.* **Kaye Umansky:** 'Foxy Down a Rabbit Hole', Copyright © Kaye Umansky 1996, first published in this collection by permission of Caroline Sheldon Literary Agency and of the author. **Celia Warren:** 'Spider's Song' and 'Pick 'N' Mix Zoo', Copyright © Celia Warren 1996, first published in this collection by permission of the author. **Clive Webster:** 'Billy-Goat Basil', 'See Me Walking' and 'When I Get Up in the Morning', Copyright © Clive Webster 1996, first published in this collection by permission of the author. **Stan Lee Werlin:** 'Ring Around the Roses', first published in *Spider* magazine, July 1994, reprinted by permission of the author.

Contents

Counting Rhymes

Finger Rhymes

Chanting Rhymes

Action Rhymes

Counting Rhymes

One, Two, I Like You

One (clap) two (clap) I like you (clap)

Two (clap) three (clap) You like me (clap)

I like Jim (clap)　　　　　I like Sue (clap)

One (clap) two (clap) I like you (clap).

Carolyn Graham

Letters

One, two, three, four –
Posting letters
Through our door.
Who's got a letter?
Who are they for?

One's for Ali.
One's for Sue.
One's for me
And one's for you!

John Foster

Five Old Fishermen

Five old fishermen
Sitting on a bridge,
One caught a tiddler
One caught a fridge.

One caught a tadpole
One caught an eel
And the fifth one caught
A pushchair wheel.

Anon

Hats

A hat for a hamster,
A hat for a dog,
A hat for a goldfish,
A hat for a frog,
A hat for me
To wear in cold weather,
How many hats
Have we got altogether?

Daphne Lister

Monsters

Five purple monsters
went out to explore.
One fell down a hole,
so that left four.

5

Four purple monsters
went down to the sea.
One swam far away,
so that left three.

4

Three purple monsters
went out to the zoo.
One joined the lions,
so that left two.

3

Two purple monsters
went out in the sun.
One got far too hot,
so that left one.

2

One purple monster
went out to have fun.
Lost his way going home,
so that left none.

1

Linda Hammond

All Good Dogs

One two three four five six seven
All good dogs will go to heaven;
Purple, yellow, green and red
All good cats will stay in bed.

Carolyn Graham

Spider's Song

One for a cobweb,
Two for the sky,
Three for a ladybird,
Four for a fly,
Five for a beetle,
Six for a bee,
Seven for a centipede
Ready for my tea.

Celia Warren

Just in time
for Tea!

Birds in the Birdcage

Birds in the birdcage
Bees in the hive,
One (clap) two (clap)
Three four five (clap).

Dogs in the doghouse
Pigs in the pen,
Six (clap) seven (clap)
Eight nine ten (clap).

Carolyn Graham

One, Two, Three, Four

One, two, three, four, Johnny hiding behind the door.

Three, four, five, six, Mammy catch him, that stop his tricks.

Six, seven, eight, nine, ten, Johnny won't do that again.

Traditional Caribbean,
adapted by John Foster

What Turkey Doing?

Mosquito one
mosquito two
mosquito jump
in de old man shoe

Cockroach three
cockroach four
cockroach dance thru
a crack in de floor

Spider five
spider six
spider weaving
a web of tricks

gobble gobble

Monkey seven
monkey eight
monkey playing with
pencil and slate

Turkey nine
turkey ten
what turkey doing
in chicken pen?

John Agard

SQUAAWK!

Beach Counting

One for the sun that shone in the sky.
Two for the ships that sailed on by.
Three for the castles I built on the sand.
Four for the seashells I held in my hand.
Five for the points on the starfish I saw.
Six for the crabs that scuttled ashore.
Seven for the waves that I managed to beat.
Eight for the pebbles I perched on my feet.
Nine for the boats that bobbed on the sea.
Ten for my toes that were wiggling free.

Tony Mitton

One Little Kitten

One little kitten
Two big cats
Three baby butterflies
Four big rats
Five fat fishes
Six sad seals
Seven silly seagulls
Eight happy eels;

Nine nervous lizards
Ten brave bees
Eleven smelly elephants
Twelve fat fleas
Thirteen alligators
Fourteen whales
Fifteen donkeys
with fifteen tails.

Carolyn Graham

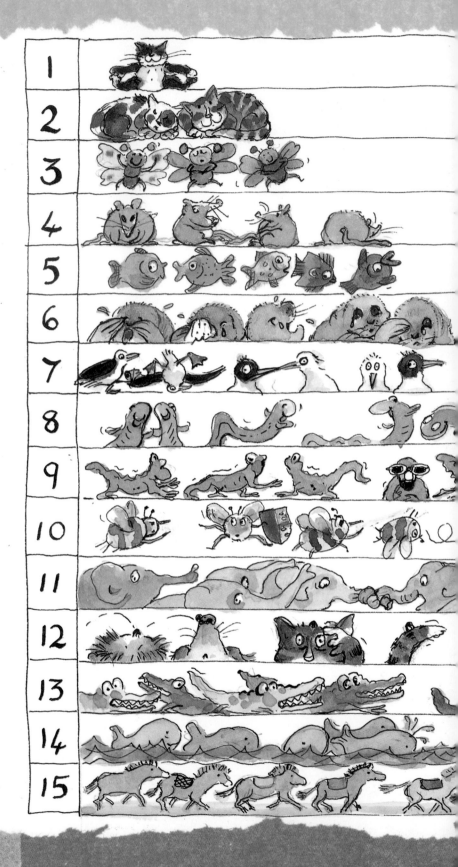

Pooh!

Countdown

Are you ready then?
We start at . . . . TEN!

We're doing fine:
The count is . . . . NINE!

The clock won't wait:
We're down to . . . . . EIGHT!

Is the next eleven?
No, silly . . . . SEVEN!

Less than two ticks
And now it's . . . . SIX!

Next we arrive
Halfway at . . . . FIVE!

Not many more:
We're down to . . . . . . FOUR!

Can't stop for tea,
The count is . . . . THREE!

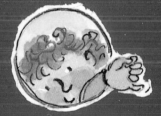

I'm scared, are you?
Yes, but it's . . . . TWO!

Time's almost gone –
We're down to . . . . ONE!

Sorry, can't stay,
It's . . . . ZERO . . . AWAY!

Eric Finney

Counting Couples

Well, Noah said, 'Roll up,
two by two.
There's room for a lot
in the floating zoo.'

So the animals came,
and they came in pairs.
They flew in the windows.
They climbed up the stairs.

2 great elephants
heavy and grey.
2 green parrots
with plenty to say.

2 big spiders
with hairy legs.
2 little sparrows
with a nest of eggs.

2 mosquitos,
2 slow snails,
2 quick squirrels
with bushy tails.

Roll up, roll up!

2 of everything
coming so fast
that Noah couldn't count
as they all rushed past.

So Noah said, 'Quick!
There's no time to lose.
If I'm going to count them all,
I'll have to count in two's.

'With a 2 and a 4
and a 6 and an 8,
hurry on in
or we're going to be late.

'2 grey mice:
that comes to 10.
2 more's 12,
with the cock and the hen.

'14, 16, 18, 20,
go on in,
there's room for plenty.
Just keep coming,
(there's no time to lose)
while I stand here
and count in two's.
Ready: 2, 4, 6, 8, 10,
12, 14, 16, 18, 20!
Who's next?'

Tony Mitton

Finger Rhymes

Five Little Fingers

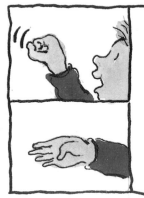

Five little fingers
Knocking on a door;
One slipped through the letter-box,
Then there were four.

Four little fingers
Climbing up a tree;
One forgot to hold on tight,
Then there were three.

Three little fingers
Eating Irish stew;
One fell in the stew pot,
Then there were two.

Two little fingers
Walking by a pond;
One slipped in the water,
Then there was one.

One little finger
Sleeping on the floor;
Woke up in the morning
And found the other four.

Jack Ousbey

Finger Play

One finger
Two fingers
Three fingers
Four,
One, two, three, four,
What are fingers for?
Pointing fingers
Crossing fingers
Grabbing fingers, too,

Stretching fingers
Hugging fingers
What else can they do?
Bending fingers
Hiding fingers
Need a thumb who's missed,
Thumb lays over
Hiding fingers –
Look!
I've made a fist!

Babs Bell Hajdusiewicz

This Finger's Straight

This finger's straight;
This finger's curled;
This one's the tallest
In the world;
This finger stands
At the end of the line;
Here's a fat thumb
And I think it's mine.

Jack Ousbey

Letter Shapes

Point with your finger.
Point to the sky.
If you put a dot on top
You can make a letter i.

Curve your thumb and finger.
Make a letter c.
It's shaped like a banana
You can eat for your tea.

Touch your thumb with your finger.
Make a letter o.
Put it round your lips
And blow, blow, blow!

John Foster

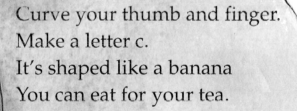

The Bird

Here are the legs
that walk along.

Here is the beak
that sings a song.

Here are the wings
that flap and spread.

And here is the bird
above my head.

Tony Mitton

Squirmy Earthworm

Squirmy, squirmy earthworm
Lives down in the ground.
But watch her wiggle out
When rain falls all around!

Squirmy, squirmy earthworm
Squirms along the ground.
But watch her disappear when
Blackbirds come around!

Babs Bell Hajdusiewicz

I'm off!

Foxy Down a Rabbit Hole

Foxy down a rabbit hole,
Looking for a bunny,
Bunny bit him on the nose,
OW! That wasn't funny!

Foxy down a mousie hole
Looking for some mice,
Mousie bit him on the nose,
OW! That wasn't nice!

Foxy down his own hole,
Lots of noisy sobbing,
Putting ointment on his nose
To try and stop it throbbing.

Kaye Umansky

Caterpillar

I can see a caterpillar
Wriggling on a leaf.

It wriggles on the top and
It wriggles underneath.

Then one day it's very still.

I stand quietly watching till
It changes shape and falls asleep.

Every day I take a peep.
Then at last, it moves about.

I'm so surprised, I give a shout.
For now there's a butterfly
Sitting on the leaf.

It spreads its wings
And flies about.

Delphine Evans

Seaside Song

Here are the cliffs.

Here are the seas.

Here are the waves
that rock in the breeze.

Here are the fishes
that dart and play.

And here are the seagulls
that fly away.

Tony Mitton

See These Fingers

See these fingers
See this hand,
Here's a crab
Walking on the sand;

Here it comes,
Watch it go,
Make sure it doesn't
Nip your toe.

Tony Langham

LOOK OUT!

Firework

Here is a sparkler.
Hold it with care.
Scribble with gold
in the cold night air.

Here are the flames
that flicker and burn.
See how they dance
as they twist and turn.

And here is a rocket
that races high.
See how it bursts
in the brilliant sky.

Tony Mitton

Arabian Nights

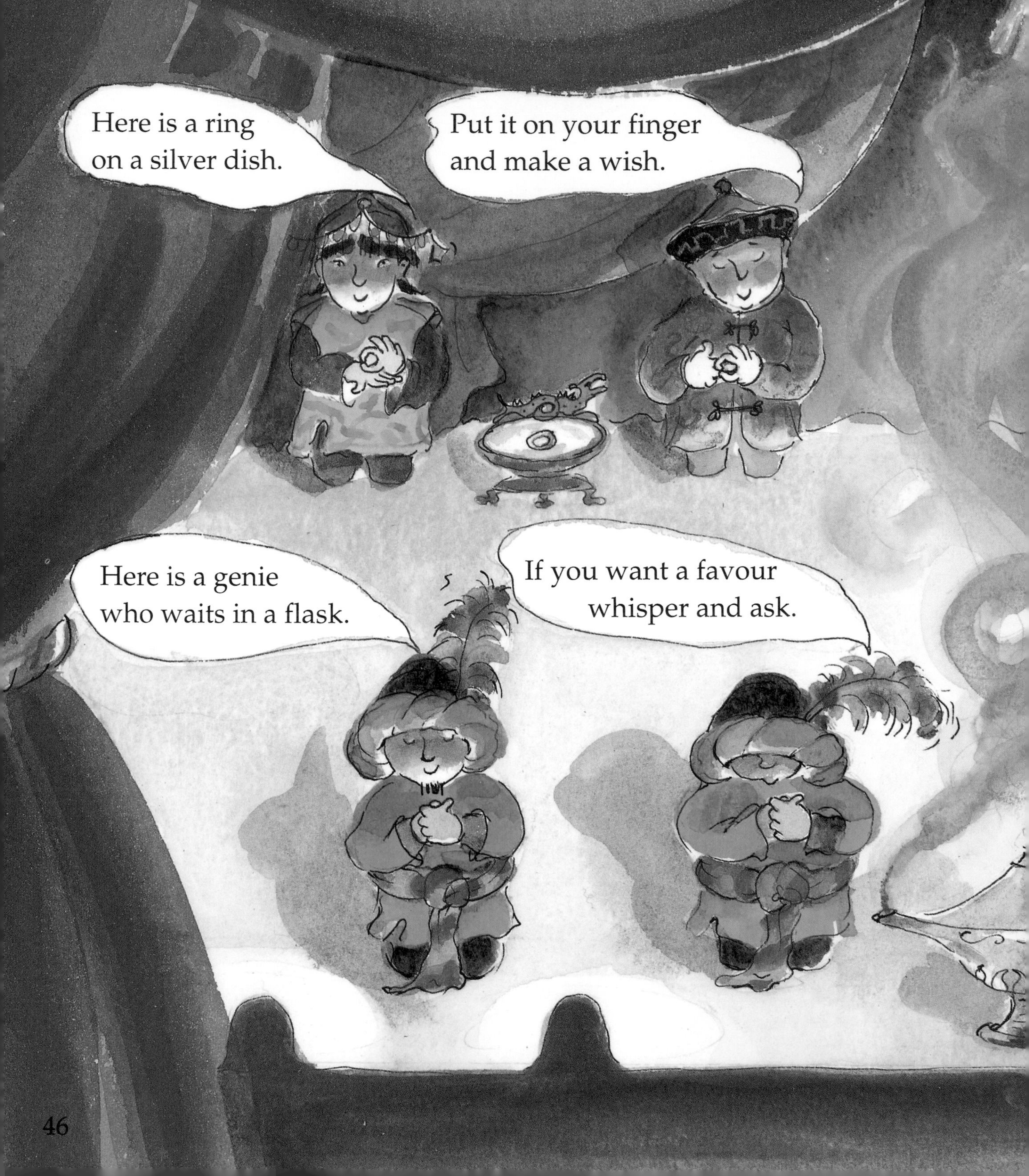

Tony Mitton

If I Had a Silver Coin

If I had a silver coin,
I'd take it to the shop

And I would buy myself a lovely
Orange lollipop.

I'd unwrap all the paper

And I'd lick and lick and lick,

And when I'd finished licking
I'd only have the stick.

I wouldn't throw it on the ground,
I wouldn't poke my brother,

I'd put it in the rubbish bin –

I wish I had another.

Wendy Cope

wheeeee

The Slide

Up the steps we're climbing,
careful not to trip.

At the top
a little hop –
Wheeeeeeeee,
down we slip!

Tony Mitton

   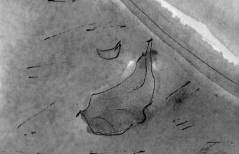

Chanting Rhymes

Marty Smarty

Marty Smarty went to a party
In her jumbo jet.
After tea she jumped in the sea
And got her pants all wet.

John Foster

Mabel Murple

Mabel Murple's house was purple
So was Mabel's hair
Mabel Murple's cat was purple
Purple everywhere.

Mabel Murple's bike was purple
So were Mabel's ears
And when Mabel Murple cried
She cried terrible purple tears.

Sheree Fitch

Ring Around the Roses

Ring around the roses
a dozen garden hoses.
Squirt you! Squirt you!
Let's all get wet!

Stan Lee Werlin

Little Amanda Sat on a Panda

Little Amanda sat on a panda,
Eating an ice-cream cone;
The panda said, 'Ouch! I'm a bear, not a couch.
Go away, please leave me alone.'

Carolyn Graham

Here a Bear, There a Bear

Here a bear, there a bear.
Everywhere there's a bear.

Bears in the hallway
Bears on the stairs

Bears under tables
Bears on chairs.

Bears in the sitting-room
Watching the telly.

Bears in the dining-room
Eating jelly.

Bears in the bathroom
Having a wash.

Bears in the kitchen
Drinking squash.

Bears in the cupboards
Bears behind doors

Bears fast asleep
On the bedroom floors.

Bears here, bears there,
There are bears everywhere.

John Foster

Billy-Goat Basil

Billy-goat Basil
And Billy-goat Ben
Butted each other
Again and again.

They butted and butted
And butted all day
Until they both butted
Each other away.

Clive Webster

58

A Chubby Little Snowman

A chubby little snowman
Had a carrot nose;
Along came a rabbit
And what do you suppose?
That hungry little bunny,
Looking for his lunch,
ATE the snowman's carrot nose . . .
Nibble, nibble, CRUNCH!

Anon

crunch!

from 'Spaghetti! Spaghetti!'

Spaghetti! spaghetti!
you're wonderful stuff,
I love you, spaghetti,
I can't get enough.
You're covered with sauce
and you're sprinkled with cheese,
spaghetti! spaghetti!
oh, give me some please.

Jack Prelutsky

60

Pick 'N' Mix Zoo

Marshmallow monkeys,
Crocodile drops,
Red jelly elephants,
Lion lollipops.

Caramel camels,
Butterscotch bears,
Toffee hippopotamus,
Chocolate hares.

Peppermint pandas,
Candy kangaroo,
Strawberry snakes
at the Pick 'n' Mix Zoo.

Celia Warren

I Don't Like Custard

I don't like custard
I don't like custard

Sometimes it's lumpy
sometimes it's thick
I don't care what it's like
It always makes me sick

I don't like custard
I don't like custard

Don't want it on my pie
don't want it on my cake
don't want it on my pudding
don't want it on my plate

I'm stuck!

I don't like custard
I don't like custard

It dribbles on the table
It dribbles on the floor
It sticks on your fingers
Then it sticks to the door

I don't like custard
I don't like custard

I can't eat it slowly
I can't eat it quick
Any way I eat it
It always makes me sick

I don't like custard
I don't like custard

Michael Rosen

down
with
Custard

I LOVE
it!

Monkey Tricks

Deep in the jungle
where the sun never shines,
see the Mighty Monkey
swinging on the vines.

Deep in the jungle
climbing up the trees,
see the Mighty Monkey
bend her hairy knees.

Deep in the jungle
where the tall tree grows,
see the Mighty Monkey
scratch her coconut nose.

Deep in the jungle
hear the drums beat,
see the Mighty Monkey
shake her dancing feet.

John Rice

Sing a Song of Popcorn

Sing a song of popcorn
When the snowstorms rage;
Fifty little round men
Put into a cage.
Shake them till they laugh and leap
Crowding to the top;
Watch them burst their little coats
Pop!! Pop!! Pop!!

Nancy Byrd Turner

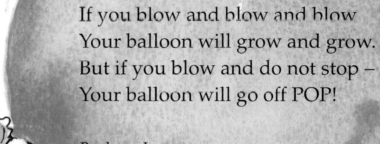

Balloon

If you blow and blow and blow
Your balloon will grow and grow.
But if you blow and do not stop –
Your balloon will go off POP!

Barbara Ireson

POP!

Children, Children

'Children, children.'
'Yes, Papa?'
'Where have you been to?'
'Grand-mamma.'
'What did she give you?'
'Bread and jam.'
'Where is my share?'
'Up in the air.'
'How can I reach it?'
'Climb on a chair.'
'Suppose I fall?'
'I don't care.'

Traditional Caribbean

Humpty Dumpty Sat on a Chair

Humpty Dumpty sat on a chair,
Eating ripe bananas.
Where do you think he put the skins?
Down his new pyjamas!

Anon

ouch!

Listen to the Tree Bear

Listen to the tree bear
Crying in the night
Crying for his mammy
In the pale moonlight.

What will his mammy do
When she hears him cry?
She'll tuck him in a cocoa-pod
And sing a lullaby.

Traditional African

Squeezes

We love to squeeze bananas.
We love to squeeze ripe plums.
And when they are feeling sad,
We love to squeeze our mums.

Brian Patten

Action Rhymes

Rocket

I am a rocket
crouched on the ground,
waiting quietly
without a sound.

Light this fuse
on my little toe . . .
Ready for take-off?
Here I go:
WOOOOOOOOOOSH!

Tony Mitton

Exercises

Bend your body,
touch your toes.

Straighten up,
and touch your nose.

Wave your arms,
now touch each knee.

Stamp your feet,
and count to three.
One, two, three!

Linda Hammond

See Me Walking

See me walking down the street,
Can you walk like me?
Walking with my head held high
As proud as can be.

See me skipping down the street,
Can you skip like this?
Throw your head back, look up high
And blow the sun a kiss.

See me jumping down the street,
Jumping oh so high.
Jump like me and stretch your arms
And try to touch the sky.

See me tip-toe down the street,
Softly on the ground.
Tip-toe tip-toe just like me,
Making not a sound.

See me hopping down the street,
Hoppety hoppety hop.
Hop with me until we're tired
And then we'll have to stop.

Clive Webster

The Robot

I am a little robot,

I come from Outer Space!

My body's made of metal
and so's my head and face.

There's lots of wires inside me
and knobs and switches too,

so if you press this button
you'll see what I can do!

I start off very slowly,
turn head from side to side,

and then my arms begin to move
out straight and then spread wide.

My legs transport me forwards, together then apart.
Clank, clank, clank, clank, clank, clank, clank,

right back to the start!

Linda Hammond

That One's Me!

Have you seen a helicopter
hover in the sky?

Have you seen a jet
go screaming by?

Have you seen a submarine
glide beneath the sea?

Have you seen a bicycle?
That one's me!

Have you seen a frog
as it hops and leaps?

Have you seen a slug
as it slowly creeps?

Have you seen a squirrel
as it scampers up a tree?

Have you seen a roly-poly?
That one's me!

Tony Mitton

The Crop Song

This is the song the seed sings: sow, sow, sow.

This is the song the shoot sings: grow, grow, grow.

This is the song the root sings: deep, deep, deep.

And this is the song the farmer sings: reap, reap, reap.

Tony Mitton

When I Get Up in the Morning

When I get up in the morning
I tumble out of bed,
I yawn and stretch and stretch and yawn
And scratch my sleepy head.

When I get up in the morning
I always wash my face,
And splash and splash the soapy water
All around the place.

When I get up in the morning
I always clean my teeth,
Front and back and back and front,
On top and underneath.

When I get up in the morning
I always brush my hair,
Brush it this way, brush it that,
Brush it everywhere.

When I get up in the morning
I always rub my tummy,
Because I know my breakfast's waiting –
Yummy yummy yummy.

Clive Webster

When Susie's Eating Custard

When Susie's eating custard,
She gets it everywhere.
Down her bib, up her nose,
All over her high chair.

She pokes it with her fingers.
She spreads it on her hair.
When Susie's eating custard,
She gets it everywhere.

John Foster

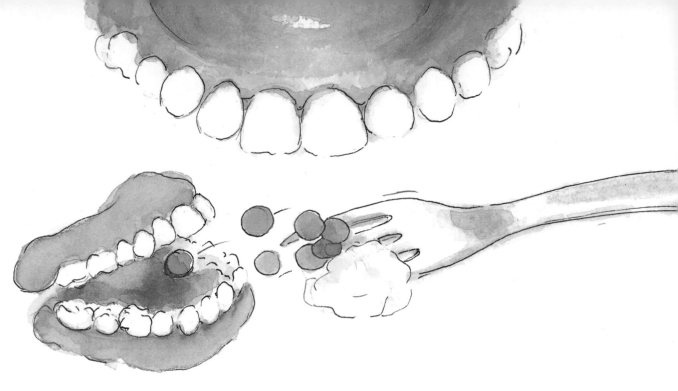

Teeth

Great big teeth,
Chomp, chomp, chomp, chomp,

Mashing up dinner,
Chomp, chomp, chomp.

If we didn't give them so much work,
Chomp, chomp, chomp, chomp,

We'd all get thinner,
Chomp, chomp, chomp.

Wendy Cope

Walking Round the Zoo

Walking round the zoo,
What did I see?

An elephant that waved
Its trunk at me.

Walking round the zoo,
What did I see?

A parrot that squawked
And winked at me.

Walking round the zoo,
What did I see?

A crocodile that snapped
Its jaws at me.

Walking round the zoo,
What did I see?

A monkey that pointed
And laughed at me!

John Foster

Three Purple Elephants

There were three purple elephants,
A little pink mouse,
A black and white panda,
A yellow wooden house.

I opened the door
Of my yellow wooden house,
Said, 'Come inside, panda.
Come inside, mouse.'

The three purple elephants said,
'What about us?'
'I'm sorry but you'll have to get
The Number Five bus.'

Joan Poulson

Lazy Little Alligator

Lazy little alligator
lying in my lap,
let me sit and stroke you
as you take a little nap.

Hungry little alligator
waking in my lap,
wonders what's for breakfast:
SNAP! SNAP! SNAP!

Tony Mitton

Dinosaur Dreams

Dinah Shore dreamed she saw
a dinosaur
peeping round her bedroom door.

Dinah Shore dreamed she saw
a dinosaur
knock on her window with its claw.

Dinah Shore dreamed she saw
a dinosaur
sleeping on the kitchen floor.

Dinah Shore dreamed she saw
a dinosaur
wake up and give a mighty ROAR!

John Foster

Creepy Crawly Creatures

At night
before I go
to sleep,
the creepy, crawly,
creatures creep.
They creep into
my bed.
And then,
they tickle
my toes
and creep
out again.

Marie Brookes

Index of Titles and First Lines

First lines are shown in italics

Index of Authors

ouch!